CHANGE YOUR

FORTUNE

365

CREATIVE STRATEGIES
TO TRANSFORM YOUR LIFE

13-Digit ISBN: 978-1-64643-016-1
10-Digit ISBN: 1-64643-016-6

This book may be ordered by mail from the publisher. Please include $5.99
for postage and handling. Please support your local bookseller first!
Books published by Cider Mill Press Book Publishers are available at special
discounts for bulk purchases in the United States by corporations, institutions,
and other organizations. For more information, please contact the publisher.

Cider Mill Press Book Publishers

"Where Good Books Are Ready for Press"
PO Box 454
12 Spring Street
Kennebunkport, Maine 04046
Visit us online!
cidermillpress.com

Typography: Brandon Grotesque, Festivo, Thistails

Printed in China
1 2 3 4 5 6 7 8 9 0
First Edition

CYF

CYF

CHANGE YOUR
FORTUNE
~ 365 ~

CREATIVE STRATEGIES
TO TRANSFORM YOUR LIFE

CYF

CYF

CIDER MILL
PRESS

BOOK
PUBLISHERS
KENNEBUNKPORT, MAINE

*I*n the effort to approach our best selves, we painstakingly develop routines and habits, dream up grand systems that will keep everything in its right place. We greedily scan the output of those who appear fully realized, hoping our search will uncover some key practice to emulate.

This appetite for control, order, and guidance causes us to lose sight of the constant change that characterizes the world we live in. Within this swirl, various specters reside— negativity, a stream of information that skews more and more extreme in every direction, attention-consuming outlets and entertainments, infinite options that are impossible navigate confidently—waiting to frustrate any momentum toward personal development. As it is never certain which one of these malevolent forces will rise against us on a particular day, our desire for reliability and structure runs into a problem—what worked yesterday may be lacking today.

In fact, it may even become another thing interested in holding you back.

Instead of a system bulked out to encompass all the world can throw at us, an enfilade of minor stratagems that can be employed and discarded as one sees fit is what is called for. Very rarely is something grand required to keep us going. Often, a small tweak or suggestion is all it takes to snap us awake, rejuvenate our imaginations, shift our perspectives, and maintain flexibility, keeping us from relying on dogma that has curdled overnight.

These creative strategies have been gathered in the hopes of meeting this call. Whether you are trying to distance yourself from the voids opened by the online world, attempting to lower the volume on naysayers without and within, or desperate for a fresh outlook, something here is bound to rise up and carry you a little further down the path.

Some of the strategies are immediately actionable. Some will require far more mulling over in order to bear fruit. Only you will know what might be worth a shot, and what you have the bandwith for. As such, it is recommended that you do not proceed through this book in a plodding, linear fashion. Flip through until you find an entry that speaks directly to the issue you are hoping to remedy, or open to a random page and act as though the first proclamation that catches your eye is your marching order for the day.

The goal of each and every prompt is not to construct an entirely new individual, but to uncover what is already within. Ultimately, fortune shifting in your favor depends on your willingness to embrace that labor.

DO BASIC, EVERYDAY TASKS
WITH YOUR WEAK HAND
FOR 3 DAYS STRAIGHT.

TAKE EVERYTHING YOU THINK
YOU NEED AND CUT IT IN HALF.

RESIST
THE URGE

TO TAKE A
PHOTO

IF YOU WANT TO DO SOMETHING,
TELL SOMEONE CLOSE TO YOU THAT
YOU'VE STARTED ON IT, AND
ARE EXCITED ABOUT IT.

MAKE YOUR HOME INTO
SOMETHING MORE THAN A MUSEUM
FOR YOUR POSSESSIONS.

REMEMBER THAT YOU DON'T HAVE
TO BE PERFECT, JUST A
LITTLE BIT BETTER EVERY DAY.

LOOK IN THE MIRROR FOR THOSE
THINGS YOU DESPISE IN OTHERS.

A MODEL IS THERE
TO GUIDE, NOT TO
RESTRICT MOVEMENT.

DEVOTE 1 DAY EVERY
2 WEEKS TO NOTHING
BUT DAYDREAMING.

FOCUS ON
DEVELOPING
MORE THAN ONE
INCOME
STREAM

CONSTANTLY ASK YOURSELF, "IS THIS THE BEST WAY TO DO THIS? HOW CAN I IMPROVE THIS PROCESS?"

BE AWARE THAT POSITIVE INVOLVEMENTS (READING, EXERCISE, ETC.) CAN EASILY TURN INTO FORMS OF PROCRASTINATION.

DON'T BE AFRAID TO CELEBRATE.
GO OUT FOR ICE CREAM OR A NICE DINNER.
DO SOMETHING THAT ALLOWS YOU TO BASK
IN THE GLOW OF YOUR TRIUMPH.

DON'T WORRY ABOUT
BEING BETTER THAN OTHERS.
FOCUS ON BECOMING THE BEST
AT BEING YOURSELF.

LEARN TO LOVE

★

SAYING NO

FIND SOMETHING SIMILAR
FROM A FOREIGN CULTURE.

GO READ SOMETHING,
ANYTHING,
BY JOHN MCPHEE.

MAKE YOUR PHYSICAL EXERCISE EACH DAY DANCING AROUND YOUR HOME FOR 30 MINUTES.

CANCEL ALL PLANS AND SPEND A WEEKEND AT HOME, DOING NOTHING MORE STRENUOUS THAN COOKING.

TAKE UP
CHESS

YOUR A-GAME ATTRACTS
PEOPLE TO YOU. THE QUALITY
OF YOUR C-GAME DETERMINES
WHO WILL REMAIN.

STOP ASSUMING THOSE IN AUTHORITY
ARE THERE BECAUSE OF ABILITY.
IT'S JUST AS LIKELY THAT THEY ARE
THERE BECAUSE THEY HAD A GOOD
10 MINUTES AT THE RIGHT TIME.

DO NOT HESITATE TO DRIFT FOLLOWING
A PERIOD OF SUSTAINED PRODUCTIVITY,
EVEN IF A DEADLINE IS LOOMING.
ANSWERS HAVE A TENDENCY TO
APPEAR DURING DOWN TIMES.

MAKE THE LAST MINUTE OF YOUR
SHOWER COLD WATER ONLY. ONCE YOU ARE
USED TO THAT, CONTINUE EXTENDING THE
LENGTH OF TIME WITHOUT HOT WATER
UNTIL THE ENTIRE SHOWER IS COLD.

SEE AN OPPORTUNITY FOR THE IMAGINATION IN SOMETHING NOT WORKING AS IT SHOULD.

EAT WHEN YOU ARE HUNGRY, RATHER THAN AT SPECIFIC POINTS OF THE DAY.

CYF

CYF

SPEND AN ENTIRE DAY SPEAKING WITH A FOREIGN ACCENT

FOCUS ON YOUR STRENGTHS

INSTEAD OF

BECOMING BALANCED

CYF

CYF

STOP TRYING TO
ALLEVIATE SADNESS OR
DISCOMFORT IMMEDIATELY.

BECOME AWARE OF YOUR
CONVERSATIONAL TICS, AND
MAKE A CONSCIOUS EFFORT
TO DO AWAY WITH THEM.

IF IT DIDN'T COME FROM
A FARM, DON'T EAT IT.

FIND A FOOLPROOF
MNEMONIC DEVICE FOR
REMEMBERING
PEOPLE'S NAMES.

MAKE THE
PHONE
CALL

★

YOU'VE BEEN
DREADING

THE
WORLD
ALWAYS APPEARS
AS THOUGH

IT IS ABOUT
TO END

CYF

CYF

DON'T WORRY ABOUT THE
NOUNS THAT DESCRIBE YOU.
FOCUS ON THE VERBS.

TOOLS ARE THERE TO CONVERT
IDEAS INTO REALITY,
NOT TO SUMMON THEM FORTH.

CULTIVATE AN HERB GARDEN. START EACH DAY BY MISTING THEM WITH WATER, AND TAKE TIME TO SIT WITH THE AROMAS THAT THEY RELEASE.

DO NOT REGRET THE CHOICES YOU HAVE MADE. RECOGNIZE THAT YOU MADE THE BEST DECISION GIVEN THE INFORMATION AVAILABLE AT THE TIME.

WHEN YOU MAKE A DECISION, NOTE YOUR REASONS FOR DOING SO AND WHAT YOUR THINKING WAS AT THE TIME. CHECK ON THESE NOTES 1 YEAR LATER AND MAKE THE NECESSARY ADJUSTMENTS IN YOUR APPROACH.

SCROLL THROUGH AN ARCHIVE OF PUBLIC DOMAIN ILLUSTRATIONS AND PHOTOS AND GATHER YOUR FAVORITES TOGETHER WITH THE INTENTION OF MAKING SOMETHING FROM THEM.

YOU CANNOT EXPECT TO BE
WHERE YOU WANT TO END UP
WHEN YOU START.

FIND A COMMUNITY AND
DO EVERYTHING YOU CAN
TO NOURISH IT.

MULTITASKING
IS SYNONYMOUS
⚡ WITH ⚡
MEDIOCRITY

Pivot

CYF

CYF

Volunteer

ASK QUESTIONS

INSTEAD OF

OFFERING ADVICE

ACKNOWLEDGE THE
DIFFERENCE BETWEEN CHEAP
AND INEXPENSIVE.

STOP SAYING YOU'RE "NOT
GOOD AT SOMETHING." INSTEAD,
SAY YOU "NEED TO IMPROVE."

Keep moving and get out of the way

Stop looking for a pattern

DON'T BE AFRAID TO
VIEW AN INVOLVEMENT
AS AN EXPERIMENT.

LISTEN TO YOUR FAVORITE
ALBUMS AT HALF-SPEED.

HEARSAY
IS NOT TO BE

ENGAGED
WITH

PLACE AN ASTERISK BESIDE ANY WORD YOU DON'T KNOW. SPEND AN HOUR LOOKING THEM UP AND COPYING THE DEFINITIONS DOWN IN A NOTEBOOK.

VIEW EVERYTHING IN THE ROOM AS AN OBJECT ONLY—WHAT DO THESE OBJECTS, AND THE ARRANGEMENT OF THEM, SAY ABOUT THE INDIVIDUALS WHO LIVE AMONGST THEM?

YOU DID NOT ALWAYS KNOW AS MUCH AS YOU DO TODAY. MEDITATE ON THIS, AND USE IT TO BECOME MORE TOLERANT OF OTHER PEOPLE, AND MORE APPRECIATIVE OF YOUR OWN ABILITIES.

THE THEORY OR NARRATIVE OF WHAT YOU ARE WORKING ON IS STRICTLY FOR OTHERS.

CYF

CYF

Treat talk as exactly that

CYF

CYF

Go swimming

BE OBNOXIOUSLY LITERAL

PUT EVERY ELEMENT
AWAY THE MINUTE YOU ARE
FINISHED USING IT.

STOP BUYING BOOKS.
INSTEAD, RE-READ THOSE
THAT HAVE MEANT THE MOST
TO YOU TO THIS POINT.

DON'T WORRY ABOUT RECEIVING CREDIT. OPERATE UNDER THE BELIEF THAT YOUR CONTRIBUTIONS WILL BE NOTICED BY SOMEONE, SOMEWHERE.

IF YOU HAVE SOMETHING YOU LIKE TO DO AND SOMEONE YOU LIKE TO LIVE WITH, YOU CAN COUNT YOURSELF AMONG THE LUCKIEST PEOPLE ON EARTH.

RECOGNIZE THAT EVEN IF YOU GET
WHAT YOU WANT, IN THE PROCESS
OF GETTING IT YOU WILL HAVE
DEVELOPED TO WHERE YOU
NO LONGER HAVE ANY USE FOR IT.

DO AS MUCH AS POSSIBLE THAT REMINDS
YOU THAT YOU ARE MORE THAN A MIND,
THAT YOU HAVE A PHYSICAL BODY.

TREAT YOUR GOOD IDEAS AS THOUGH
THEY HAVE AN EXPIRATION DATE,
JUST AS A GALLON OF MILK DOES.

YOU WILL NOT FEEL LIKE DOING THOSE
THINGS YOU NEED TO UNTIL
YOU ARE 10 TO 20 MINUTES INTO THEM.

HOW IS THE ROOM WHERE YOU
WORK AFFECTING THE SHAPE
OF THE THINGS YOU PRODUCE?

BELIEVE THAT, GIVEN ENOUGH TIME
AND ATTENTION, YOU COULD POSSESS THE
VERY SAME ABILITIES YOU ENVY IN
OTHERS IN NO MORE THAN 6 MONTHS.

GIVE YOURSELF A PRESENT

★

EVERY DAY

KEEP A WATCHFUL EYE FOR
THINGS TO STEAL
AND MAKE YOUR OWN.

DO NOT ADD. SUBTRACT
HABITS AND DISREGARD
INCLINATIONS UNTIL YOU
BEGIN TO FEEL BETTER.

MAKE SURE YOUR OWN
HOUSE IS IN ORDER BEFORE
TENDING TO OTHERS.

IS MAINTAINING YOUR
SYSTEM SUCKING UP MORE
ENERGY THAN IT SAVES?

BEWARE

OF

PRETTY THINKING

AVOID
SUGAR

AS MUCH AS
POSSIBLE

GO OUTSIDE AND BE IN
THE SUNLIGHT WITHIN AN
HOUR OF WAKING UP.

KEEP A CLEAR DIVISION
BETWEEN YOUR PUBLIC
AND PRIVATE LIVES.

OPERATE AS THOUGH ONLY 15 MINUTES IN A GIVEN YEAR WILL END UP BEING OF CONSEQUENCE. SPEND YOUR ENERGY POSITIONING YOURSELF TO THRIVE IN THOSE MOMENTS.

HOW YOU GET ALONG WITH OTHERS IS A MUCH BIGGER FACTOR IN YOUR OVERALL SUCCESS THAN TALENT OR INTELLIGENCE.

BECOME MORE COMFORTABLE ASKING:
HOW DOES THIS AFFECT THE SYSTEM
IN WHICH IT EXISTS?

KEEP A FILE OF INTERESTING OR
INSPIRING QUOTATIONS ON YOUR COMPUTER.
START EACH DAY BY PICKING A PAGE AT
RANDOM AND LOOKING THROUGH IT.

CYF

CYF

Floss at least once a day

Keep a dream journal

ALLOW YOURSELF ONE INVOLVEMENT
WHERE YOU CAN BE
AS RUTHLESS AS POSSIBLE.

REFRAME EVERY CRITICISM OR SLIGHT
UNTIL IT IS AN INDICATION
THAT YOU ARE ON THE RIGHT PATH.

START THE DAY WITH WHATEVER
ALLOWS YOU TO BUILD MOMENTUM.

TRY TO ELIMINATE AS
MANY OPTIONS AS YOU CAN.

STOP QUALIFYING YOUR APOLOGIES.
SIMPLY SAY SORRY, SPECIFY WHAT FOR,
AND LEAVE IT AT THAT.

BE MORE WILLING TO
RATIONALIZE THE ACTIONS OF
OTHERS THAN YOUR OWN.

COPY SOMETHING YOU LOVE WORD FOR WORD, LINE FOR LINE, NOTE FOR NOTE UNTIL IT IS INGRAINED.

LEAVE SPACES AND PROCEED, TRUSTING THAT THE ANSWERS WILL COME LATER SO LONG AS YOU MAINTAIN MOMENTUM.

STOP COMPLAINING

AND FIND A SOLUTION

AVOID ANYTHING THAT REQUIRES STRICT ADHERENCE IN ORDER TO PROVE EFFECTIVE.

BECOME MORE COMFORTABLE WITH BEING THE DUMBEST PERSON IN THE ROOM.

MEDITATE ON WHAT YOU
WANT TO LET GO OF.

DON'T FIGHT BACK AGAINST
SOMEONE WHO IS ANGRY.

RECOGNIZE WHAT THE WORD "WANT" ACTUALLY MEANS AND CONDUCT YOURSELF ACCORDINGLY.

KEEP A LIST OF THOSE THINGS YOU HAVE HIDDEN.

LOOK FOR THE
ONE GOOD
THING
AND MAKE
SOMETHING
BIG OF IT

TRY CBD OIL AND
OTHER RELATED PRODUCTS
FOR 1 MONTH.

WHAT ELSE DOES THE CHANGE
YOU WANT TO MAKE AFFECT?

BELIEVE THAT YOU ARE
RESPONSIBLE FOR EVERYTHING
THAT HAPPENS IN YOUR LIFE.

REMOVE YOUR MIND FROM
THE EQUATION, AND SIMPLY
BE AN ATHLETE.

WHAT'S THE
WORST

THAT CAN
HAPPEN

CYF

CYF

SQUINT AND SEE WHAT POPS OUT. DEPENDING ON WHAT YOU WANT, EITHER TONE DOWN OR AMPLIFY THAT ELEMENT.

TO INCREASE THE SPEED OF SOMETHING AND HAVE IT REMAIN EFFECTIVE, THE KEY IS NOT MOVING FASTER, BUT IDENTIFYING WHICH COMPONENTS CAN BE REMOVED.

TRY AND REMEMBER THE LAST TIME YOU
CONVINCED SOMEONE OF SOMETHING
WITH NOTHING MORE THAN PURE REASON.

ACCEPT THAT YOU WILL NEVER
ARRIVE. THERE WILL ALWAYS BE
SOMETHING BEYOND WHAT YOU
BELIEVE TO BE THE FINISH LINE.

Spend a day alone in a museum

CYF

CYF

Refuse to keep score

MAKE SOMETHING YOU WOULD TYPICALLY PURCHASE AT THE STORE—PASTA, ICE CREAM, A ROASTED CHICKEN, HUMMUS, ETC.

IF YOUR COMMUTE IS LONGER THAN 20 MINUTES EACH WAY, FIGURE SOMETHING ELSE OUT.

GET COMFORTABLE WITH THE DISTANCE
THAT EXISTS BETWEEN THE IMAGE
IN YOUR MIND AND REALITY.

CONSIDER HOW YOU WOULD ACT IF
YOU KNEW YOU ONLY HAD 6 MONTHS
LEFT TO LIVE, AND MAKE THE
NECESSARY ADJUSTMENTS.

DO NOT
TOLERATE
THE
INTOLERANT

CYF

CYF

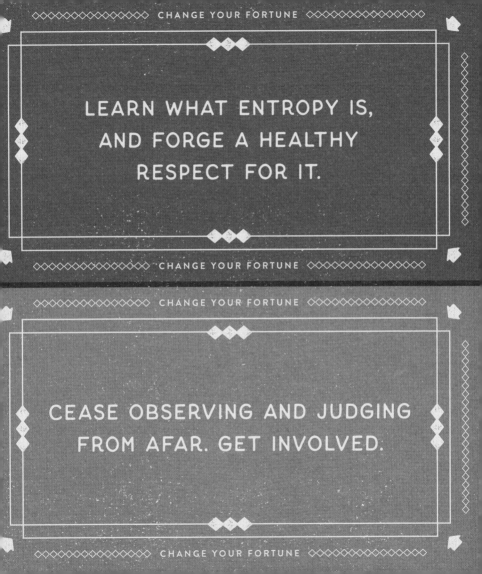

LEARN WHAT ENTROPY IS, AND FORGE A HEALTHY RESPECT FOR IT.

CEASE OBSERVING AND JUDGING FROM AFAR. GET INVOLVED.

READ SOMETHING YOU
LOVE OUT LOUD TO
SOMEONE YOU LOVE.

IF YOU CAN EXPLAIN
EXACTLY WHAT YOU DID,
THE RESULT CAN BE GOOD,
BUT NEVER GREAT.

LEARN SOMETHING NEW EVERY DAY

STOP
ONLY WHEN
YOU KNOW
WHAT TO DO
NEXT

CYF

CYF

FIND A METAPHOR FOR ANYTHING THAT GRABS YOUR ATTENTION.

GET AWAY FROM THE WINTER FOR 2 WEEKS.

HIGHLIGHT, INSTEAD OF HIDE,
YOUR REFERENCES AND INFLUENCES.

TAKE A CLASS IN SOMETHING
YOU'VE ALWAYS LOVED BUT BELIEVED
YOU HAD NO FACILITY FOR.

SPEND 1 YEAR FOCUSING YOUR
SPARE TIME ON CULTIVATING A GARDEN.

PRETENSION CAN PROVIDE A PATH
TO ERUDITION AND ENLIGHTENMENT.

IS THE LAST-MINUTE IMPROVEMENT GOOD ENOUGH TO MAKE UP FOR THE INCREASED CHANCE OF ERROR?

FEEDBACK IS THERE TO CLARIFY. VIEW IT AS THE TREMENDOUS GIFT THAT IT IS.

THAT WHICH SEEMS TO VANQUISH IS
ALSO LIBERATING IF VIEWED
FROM A DIFFERENT PERSPECTIVE.

LEAVE SOME SPACE BETWEEN YOU AND
SOMETHING YOU LOVE, SO THAT EACH
ENCOUNTER WITH IT WILL BE CHARGED
WITH SOME OF THE INITIAL MAGIC.

FIGURE OUT WHO TO PAY ATTENTION TO UPON ENTERING AN UNFAMILIAR SPACE.

LISTEN TO NOTHING ON YOUR DRIVE TO OR FROM WORK.

JUST GET SOMETHING DOWN AND GO TO SLEEP, TRUSTING THAT YOUR UNCONSCIOUS WILL WORK IT INTO SHAPE.

GIVE ACUPUNCTURE A TRY.

LEARN TO READ

CYF CYF

THE ROOM

FIGURE OUT WHO INFLUENCED
YOUR INFLUENCES.

CEASE JUDGING SOMEONE'S
INSIDES BY WHAT IS OUTSIDE.

ASPIRE TO SURRENDER
WHILE REMAINING ACTIVE.

IMAGINE EVERYTHING YOU
THROW AWAY FLOATING
IN THE BODY OF WATER
CLOSEST TO YOUR HOUSE.

WAIT TWO SECONDS

STOP SAYING YOU'VE SEEN SOMETHING OR READ SOMETHING SIMPLY TO BE AGREEABLE OR SEEM WITH IT.

THOSE WHO HOLD AUTHORITY AND PROVE THEMSELVES TO BE INCAPABLE OF IT SHOULD NOT BE TRUSTED UNDER ANY CIRCUMSTANCES.

TRAIN YOURSELF TO HAVE ALARM BELLS
GO OFF EVERY TIME YOU OR SOMEONE
ELSE SAYS THE WORD "SHOULD."

DONE IS ALMOST
ALWAYS BETTER THAN GOOD.

SOMETHING HAS TO BE WORTH

DYING FOR

RECOGNIZE THE IMPULSE
TO LIE AS WHAT IT IS:
A SIGN THAT YOU DON'T
TRUST THE OTHER PERSON.

REDUCE YOUR INTENDED
AUDIENCE TO ONE PERSON AND
TRY TO PLEASE ONLY THEM.

STOP PLACING YOURSELF
AT THE CENTER OF
EVERY ENGAGEMENT.

CEDE TO THE
SERENDIPITY THAT AN
"ERROR" CAN PROVIDE.

IF YOU LOST IT, IT WAS NEVER REALLY YOURS

Rebrand the situation as a farce

Almost everything can be learned

CYF

TEACH YOURSELF TO PLAY THE PIANO

CYF

DON'T ALLOW YOURSELF TO EXIST STRICTLY ON PAPER.

ORGANIZE YOUR LIFE SO THAT A CALENDAR OR A DAY PLANNER IS NOT NECESSARY.

FOCUS LESS ON WHAT MAKES IT NEW
AND MORE ON WHAT MAKES IT WORK.

SHOULD THE THING YOU ENDED UPON
BE MOVED UP TO THE BEGINNING?

OPEN THE FANCIEST COOKBOOK YOU HAVE AND ATTEMPT TO MAKE THE MOST INTIMIDATING RECIPE IN IT. REPEAT UNTIL IT IS GOOD ENOUGH TO SERVE TO COMPANY.

VIEW YOUR LIFE AS AN OPPORTUNITY RATHER THAN A SERIES OF THINGS THAT HAPPENS TO YOU.

WHEN YOU REACH FOR A NEARBY
SWEATER OR A BLANKET TO RELIEVE
A CHILL, LET THE INCREDIBLE FORTUNE
THAT ENABLES YOU TO DO SO SINK IN.

REDEFINE THOSE WORDS THAT FEEL
THE MOST ALIVE TO YOU
UNTIL THEY ARE ENTIRELY YOURS.

WHEN YOU FIND YOURSELF WITH
5 SPARE MINUTES,
DON'T REACH FOR YOUR PHONE.

START KEEPING TRACK OF HOW
MANY TIMES A DAY YOU INTERRUPT
SOMEONE, AND WHO IT IS THAT
YOU ARE INTERRUPTING.

WHY IS THE ROOM SET
UP THIS WAY, AND
NOT SOME OTHER WAY?

VOICE THOSE THINGS
YOU BELIEVE TO GO
WITHOUT SAYING.

DON'T HESITATE

TO

SHOW OFF

A LITTLE

FORGIVENESS IS THE ONLY
WAY TO FREE YOURSELF
FROM THE PAST.

YOU ALREADY HAVE
ENOUGH INFORMATION.

SPEND AN HOUR WATCHING
BUSTER KEATON CLIPS.

CHAMPION ONLY THOSE
VIRTUES WHICH YOU PRACTICE
WITHIN YOUR CIRCLE.

ACT UPON ANY KIND GESTURE
THAT POPS INTO YOUR HEAD.

FOCUS ON YOUR BREATHING—NOT SO
MUCH REMINDING YOURSELF TO BREATHE,
BUT ON HOW EACH BREATH FEELS.

TREAT YOURSELF AND A FRIEND
TO CHAMPAGNE RISOTTO.

ENTERTAIN THE POSSIBILITY THAT THOSE
WHO INSTILLED BELIEFS IN YOU
MAY NOT HAVE SEEN ENOUGH OF THE
WORLD FOR THOSE BELIEFS TO
CARRY THE WEIGHT THAT THEY DO.

WHEN YOU START TO FEEL UNAPPRECIATED, PAY ATTENTION TO HOW WELL YOU'VE SLEPT AND HOW YOU'VE EATEN FOR THE PAST WEEK.

SPEND 30 MINUTES WATCHING BALLET DANCERS.

UNDERSTAND THAT BECOMING ANNOYED HAS FAR MORE TO DO WITH YOU THAN WHATEVER THE "OFFENDER" IS DOING.

WHEN YOU FIND YOURSELF MAKING A NEGATIVE JUDGMENT ABOUT SOMEONE, FIND A WAY TO GIVE THEM THE BENEFIT OF THE DOUBT.

LET GO OF YOUR MEMORIES OF
A PLACE WHEN PASSING THROUGH IT.

FEAR RESULTING FROM ANYTHING
NON-LETHAL IS SIMPLY TELLING YOU
WHAT YOU NEED TO MOVE TOWARD.

SPEND AN HOUR
IN CANDLELIGHT
EVERY EVENING.

REARRANGE YOUR BEDROOM.

DEADLINES
⚡ ARE ⚡
ESSENTIAL

READ THE NEWSPAPER WITH
THE PERSPECTIVE THAT EACH STORY
IS IN FACT A PRESS RELEASE.

MAKE A CONSCIOUS EFFORT TO DO THINGS
WITHOUT BRINGING YOUR PHONE ALONG.

THE DESIRE FOR FAME AND RECOGNITION IS A SICKNESS THAT NEEDS TO BE ELIMINATED BEFORE YOU CAN PRODUCE ANYTHING OF VALUE.

LOOK FOR THE EXAMPLES THAT DISPROVE YOUR THEORY.

CYF

CYF

CUT OUT

THE

BOOZE

SEARCH UNTIL YOU LAND
UPON THE MYTHIC ASPECT
OF AN EXPERIENCE.

TRY TO TIE EVERYTHING TO
A PHYSICAL PHENOMENON.

NO MATTER WHAT,
EVERYONE BELIEVES THEY
ARE DOING THEIR BEST.

IMAGES ARE FOR THE MASSES.
WORDS ARE FOR THE INDIVIDUAL.

WHAT WOULD BE DIFFERENT IF
YOU GREW UP ON A FARM IN KANSAS?
ON THE OCEAN IN MAINE?

WHAT CAN YOU REUSE?

FOR SOMETHING TO BE GOOD,
SOME RULE HAS TO BE BROKEN.

TURN OFF ALL NOTIFICATIONS
REGARDING ACTIVITY ONLINE.

ACT AS THOUGH YOUR ANCESTORS
ARE HANGING ON YOUR EVERY MOVE.

DO YOU WANT 10 TIMES
MORE OF THIS IN YOUR LIFE?

HONOR THE THINGS YOU SAY WHEN
YOU'RE FEELING A LITTLE TIPSY.

SPEND TOO MUCH MONEY ON
SOMETHING YOU HAVE BEEN WANTING
TO DO BUT PUTTING OFF.

GET A SLOW COOKER, FIND FIVE
RECIPES YOU LIKE FOR IT, AND
COMMIT TO MAKING ONE A WEEK.

ONCE A WEEK, PICK UP
SOMEONE'S—A FRIEND'S,
A STRANGER'S—TAB
IN A RESTAURANT.

BECOME OK WITH LEAVING THINGS UNRESOLVED.

USE A FOREIGN MATERIAL.

VISUALIZE HOW YOU
WANT SOMETHING TO GO
BEFORE IT HAPPENS.

BE BETTER ABOUT
FOLLOWING UP.

CONSIDER THE STRUCTURE OF THE THING
WHEN DECIDING WHERE TO GO NEXT.

SKIP BREAKFAST, CONSUMING NOTHING BUT
BLACK COFFEE AND WATER UNTIL LUNCH.

TIME SPENT PLANNING IS MORE VALUABLE
THAN THE RESULTING PLAN.

BREAK LARGER TASKS INTO THE SMALLER
COMPONENTS THAT MAKE THEM UP.

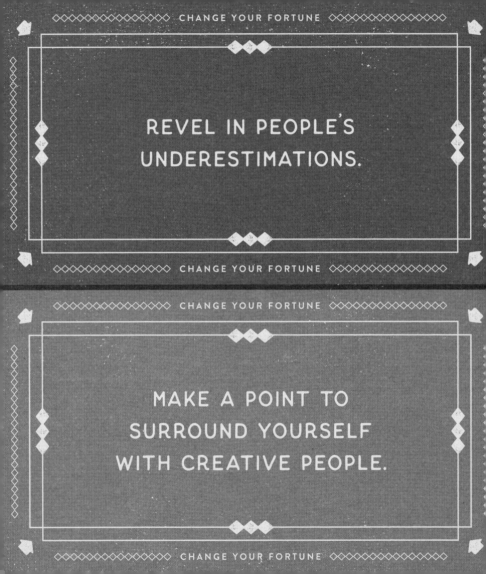

REVEL IN PEOPLE'S
UNDERESTIMATIONS.

MAKE A POINT TO
SURROUND YOURSELF
WITH CREATIVE PEOPLE.

ARE YOU JUST TRYING
TO MAKE IT ABOUT YOU?

NEEDING MORE THAN ONE REASON
TO DO SOMETHING IS A
SIGN YOU SHOULDN'T DO IT.

WATCH FOR WHAT PEOPLE ARE COMMUNICATING WITH THEIR PREFERENCES, RATHER THAN WHAT THEY ARE PROFFERING.

SHIFT THE PERIOD OF REFLECTION TO AFTER THE ACTION, RATHER THAN DURING IT.

TRY TO FILL SOME PORTION OF EACH DAY WITH IDEAS THAT CHALLENGE WHAT YOU HOLD TO BE TRUE.

FIND A 10-MINUTE SERIES OF STRETCHES, AND DO THEM EVERY MORNING FOR A MONTH.

STAY OUT OF THE ECHO CHAMBERS AVAILABLE TO YOU.

REPEAT SOMETHING UNTIL IT STARTS TO FEEL COMPLETELY ALIEN.

FLIP A COIN. WHEN IT REACHES ITS APEX, PAY ATTENTION TO WHAT SIDE YOU ARE ROOTING FOR. DO NOT EVEN LOOK AT WHAT SIDE IT LANDS ON, FOR YOU ALREADY KNOW WHAT YOU WANT TO DO.

REMEMBER THAT ALMOST EVERYTHING YOU DO WILL SEEM IMPOSSIBLY SILLY IN THE FUTURE, AND CARRY THE RESULTING LIGHTNESS WITH YOU EACH TIME YOU MAKE A DECISION.

GO THROUGH YOUR POSSESSIONS.
ANYTHING YOU WOULD BE DEVASTATED TO
LOSE IF THE HOUSE CAUGHT ON FIRE, KEEP.
EVERYTHING ELSE, DONATE OR SELL.

REFLECT ON WHAT WAS HAPPENING
ON THIS DATE 1 YEAR AGO.
HOW HAVE YOU PROGRESSED?

WHEN WALKING AROUND, DON'T FORGET
TO LOOK UP FROM TIME TO TIME.

ACT AS THOUGH THIS IS THE LAST
TIME YOU WILL ENCOUNTER
A PARTICULAR PERSON OR PLACE.

PICK UP A BOOK AND START READING. STOP AT THE FIRST THING THAT STRIKES YOUR FANCY, AND ACT AS THOUGH IT IS AN INSTRUCTION FROM THE DIVINE.

BEFORE WHACKING A SPIDER OR A BUG, CONSIDER THE DYNAMIC THAT IS AT PLAY.

BE MORE GIVING

MORE GENEROUS

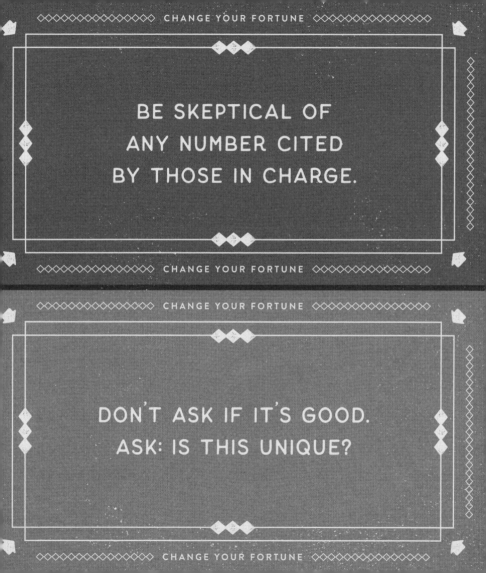

BE SKEPTICAL OF
ANY NUMBER CITED
BY THOSE IN CHARGE.

DON'T ASK IF IT'S GOOD.
ASK: IS THIS UNIQUE?

IT IS BETTER TO MAKE A DECISION
AND HAVE TO IMPROVISE LATER
THAN TO WAIT AROUND UNTIL
CERTAINTY ARRIVES.

MAKE A TO-DO LIST EACH DAY
WITH THREE THINGS YOU ABSOLUTELY
HAVE TO GET DONE. ONCE YOU HAVE THEM
CROSSED OFF, THE REST OF THE DAY
CAN BE SPENT HOWEVER YOU LIKE.

PICK THREE PEOPLE IN YOUR LIFE AND SCHEDULE A PHONE CALL WITH THEM EVERY MONTH.

SPEND SUNDAY EVENING PREPARING YOUR MEALS FOR THE WEEK, WITH SOME GOOD MUSIC AND A GLASS OR TWO OF WINE FOR COMPANY.

BE LESS TIED TO WORKING
IN CHRONOLOGICAL ORDER.

BE WARY OF ANYTHING
THAT ALLOWS YOU TO
"TURN OFF YOUR MIND."

STOP MAKING SENSE

CYF

CYF

MAKE IT YOUR OWN

FREE LABOR IS AT THE
ROOT OF EVERYTHING THAT
RETAINS ITS VALUE.

TRY MAKING MORE, RATHER
THAN PINCHING PENNIES.

WHEN YOU FIND YOURSELF GETTING
ANXIOUS OR ANGRY, TRY TO
SOLVE WHAT'S CAUSING THE ISSUE
THROUGH COMMUNICATION.

START TO SCHEDULE PERIODS
OF FREE TIME, AND ALLOW
YOURSELF TO DO WHATEVER SEEMS
APPEALING IN THAT MOMENT.

LOOK AROUND YOUR ROOM.
TOSS EVERYTHING THAT'S MEANING
IS NOT IMMEDIATELY APPARENT
INTO A TRASH CAN.

TRY TO BREAK YOUR CONDITIONING.
TAKE DIFFERENT ROUTES TO PLACES
YOU FREQUENTLY TRAVEL TO. SET YOUR
ALARM FOR DIFFERENT TIMES.
GO A DAY WITHOUT COFFEE.

Stop privileging the effortless

CHANGE YOUR FORTUNE

CYF

Get a space that is solely yours

CYF

CHANGE YOUR FORTUNE

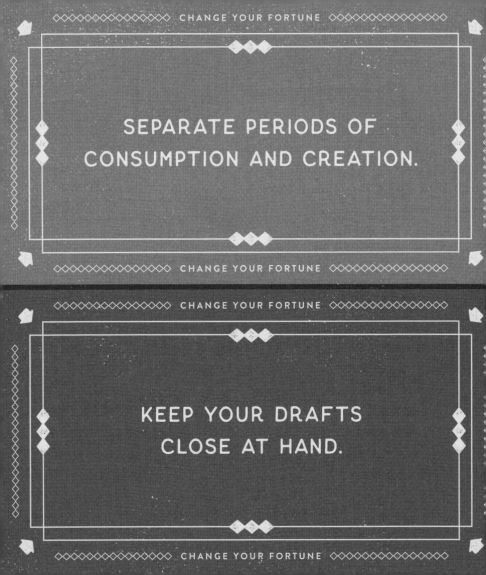

SEPARATE PERIODS OF
CONSUMPTION AND CREATION.

KEEP YOUR DRAFTS
CLOSE AT HAND.

DRAW IT

DON'T RUSH TO FILL THE SILENCE WHEN ONE ARISES DURING A CONVERSATION.

VIEW EVERY DETOUR OR DEVIATION FROM THE ROUTE AS A POTENTIAL LIFESAVER.

SCROLL THROUGH YOUR BOOKMARKS AND SPEND SOME TIME WITH THOSE THAT AREN'T IMMEDIATELY FAMILIAR.

EVEN THE SMARTEST PEOPLE HAVE A NUMBER OF AREAS WHERE THEY SOUND STUPID.

ANTICIPATION

IS AKIN TO

BLINDNESS

IT'S EASY TO TELL EVERYONE
HOW GOOD YOU ARE.
WHEN YOU'RE REALLY GOOD,
THEY'LL TELL YOU.

SIT AND WATCH THE
OCEAN FOR A HALF-HOUR.

EVERYONE BUT THE ARTIST IS FORCED TO SPECIALIZE.

EXPLORE YOUR TOOLS UNTIL YOU HAVE EXHAUSTED ALL THAT THEY ARE CAPABLE OF.

IF YOU NEED TO MAKE SURE YOU BRING SOMETHING ALONG, PLACE YOUR PHONE IN THE CENTER OF A TABLE AND PLACE THE ESSENTIAL ITEM ON TOP OF IT.

STOP READING THE NEWSPAPER. CEASE WATCHING THE NIGHTLY NEWS. UNDERSTAND THAT YOU WILL ENCOUNTER THOSE THINGS YOU NEED TO BE AWARE OF SIMPLY BY MOVING THROUGH THE WORLD.

LISTEN ONLY TO
INSTRUMENTALS
WHILE WORKING.

DON'T BE AFRAID TO HAVE
STANDARDS, TO SEEM FANCY.

EVERYTHING
HAS A COST
EVERYTHING

MEDITATE ON THE DIFFERENCE
BETWEEN WITNESSING AND WATCHING
UNTIL YOU CAN FEEL IT.

DO WHATEVER THE COMPLETE OPPOSITE
OF WHAT YOU'VE BEEN DOING IS.

**CHARLATANS LOVE TO SELL THE
ILLUSION OF CONSTANT GROWTH.**

**SURRENDER YOUR AUTONOMY
WHEN IN PUBLIC.**

COMPLEXITY IS FOR YOUR OWN ENTERTAINMENT, NOT TO DAZZLE OTHERS.

GIVE PEOPLE A CHANCE TO TELL THEIR STORIES.

COME UP WITH AN INVOCATION TO THE MUSES

Don't be afraid to repeat yourself

CHANGE YOUR FORTUNE

CYF

If you can't eat it, don't buy it

CYF

CHANGE YOUR FORTUNE

SAY YES TO EVERY PARTY YOU ARE INVITED TO

CYF

CYF

TRY APPLYING A CONCEPT
THAT WORKS IN ONE ARENA
TO EVERYTHING ELSE
YOU ARE INVOLVED IN.

ADVERTISING IS NOT NECESSARY
FOR THOSE THINGS THAT
ARE GOOD ENOUGH TO STAND
ON THEIR OWN MERIT.

Make a list

MEDITATE AS YOU LAY IN
BED TO GO TO SLEEP.

GIVE YOUR FULL ATTENTION
TO EVERYTHING YOU DO,
NO MATTER HOW MUNDANE.

THERE IS
NO SUCH
THING
AS THE
PERFECT
TIME

MAKE VEGETABLES A PART OF EVERY MEAL

GIVE PEOPLE A REASON
TO STICK AROUND
AND HEAR THE THEORY.

MORE COMPLEX VERY
RARELY MEANS BETTER.

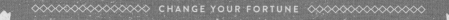
SELECT THREE PRIORITIES AND
SAY NO TO EVERYTHING
THAT FALLS OUTSIDE OF THEM.

WHEN READING, WRITE OUT
WHAT YOU'VE LEARNED AS
THOUGH YOU WERE PREPARING
A LECTURE ABOUT IT.

CHANGE YOUR FORTUNE

CYF

CYF

LEAVE YOUR PHONE IN ANOTHER ROOM

CHANGE YOUR FORTUNE

Leave one mistake in

CYF

CYF

Construct a mind palace

WHAT DOES SUCCESS LOOK LIKE HERE?
IF YOU CANNOT ANSWER THAT
QUESTION, RE-EXAMINE THE PROJECT.

VIEW TIME ALONE AS A GIFT RATHER
THAN A MISFORTUNE TO BE ENDURED.

SCOUR THRIFT STORES AND USED BOOKSTORES FOR CHEAP ART BOOKS AND KEEP THEM AROUND YOUR WORKSPACE. WHEN YOU FEEL STUCK, UNINSPIRED, OR ADRIFT, SIT WITH A CUP OF TEA AND FLIP THROUGH THEM.

CONSIDERABLE EFFORTS MADE IN REVISION ARE NECESSARY TO PRODUCE THE APPEARANCE OF EFFORTLESSNESS.

STOP EXPECTING THAT
THINGS WILL BE FAIR.

INSTEAD OF WAITING FOR SOMEONE TO
SAY "YES," MAKE YOUR OWN PLATFORM.

FIND AN IMAGE THAT PREVENTS
YOU FROM DRIFTING.

BECOME MORE INTERESTED
IN DOING THAN DOCUMENTING.

REMOVE EVERYTHING THAT
DOES NOT FEEL ALIVE.

MINE WHAT YOU HAVE
INSTEAD OF SEARCHING
FOR NEW CONTENT.

FAILURE
IS ALWAYS AN OPTION

IT IS ALSO FAR FROM
DISASTROUS

GET COMFORTABLE WITH DOING NOTHING

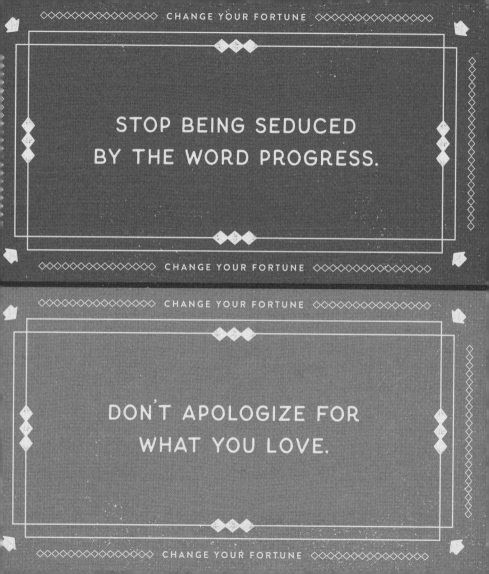

STOP BEING SEDUCED
BY THE WORD PROGRESS.

DON'T APOLOGIZE FOR
WHAT YOU LOVE.

FOR 1 MONTH, NO MATTER WHAT
IS LEFT ON YOUR TO-DO LIST,
GO TO BED THE MOMENT
YOU BEGIN TO FEEL DROWSY.

HAVING FINAL SAY IS ALMOST
ALWAYS WORTH MORE
THAN ANY AMOUNT OF MONEY.

ADD A PAPER TOWEL SCENTED
WITH A FEW DROPS OF YOUR
FAVORITE FRAGRANCE TO THE DRYER
ALONG WITH YOUR WET CLOTHES.

BE CAREFUL ABOUT TURNING
THOSE THINGS THAT BRING
YOU JOY INTO YOUR JOB.

AGREE TO AN AMOUNT OF TIME
RATHER THAN AN ENTIRE PROJECT.

SPEND 5 MINUTES LOOKING AT
THE LIGHT IN THE ROOM YOU
ARE IN, AND HOW QUICKLY
IT CEDES TO SHADOW.

CHANGING IS AS SIMPLE, AND AS DIFFICULT, AS CONSISTENTLY CHOOSING TO DEPRIVE YOUR PRESENT INCLINATIONS OF OXYGEN.

PAY MORE ATTENTION TO YOUR PERSONAL STYLE. TREAT IT AS THOUGH IT IS THE ONLY WAY TO COMMUNICATE WHO YOU BELIEVE YOURSELF TO BE TO OTHERS.

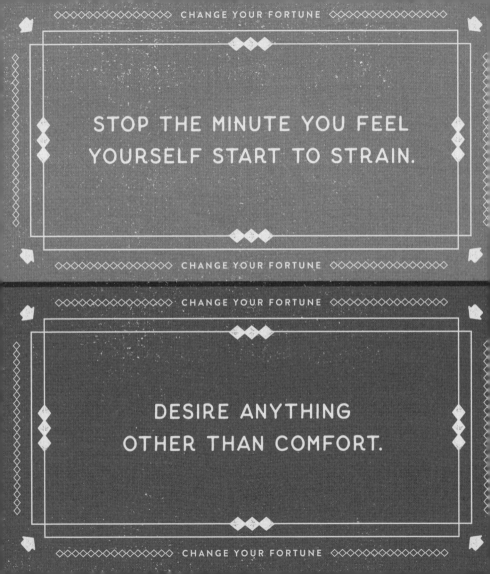

STOP THE MINUTE YOU FEEL YOURSELF START TO STRAIN.

DESIRE ANYTHING OTHER THAN COMFORT.

OPEN A WINDOW

THOSE WHO "BURST ONTO THE SCENE"
HAVE BEEN STEADILY WORKING
THEIR WAY THERE FOR DECADES.

SET A REMINDER TO LOOK THROUGH
YOUR FAMILY PHOTOS ONCE A MONTH.

WRITE A LETTER TO A LOVED ONE TRYING TO EXPLAIN THE NATURE OF WHAT YOU ARE STUCK ON TO THEM.

IF YOU CAN DO IT WITH THE TV ON, IT IS NOT WORTH DOING AT ALL.

"CLAIR DE LUNE" IS 4 MINUTES LONG.
DEBUSSY WORKED ON IT FOR 20 YEARS.

ACT AS THOUGH THE FIRST STEP
IS A COMPLETE COMMITMENT,
NEVER TO BE QUESTIONED.

CONCLUDE EACH DAY BY LISTING OFF THE THINGS THAT YOU ARE GRATEFUL FOR.

BUY A DICTIONARY. READ TWO PAGES A DAY AND WRITE DOWN THE WORDS THAT CATCH YOUR EYE, AS WELL AS THEIR DEFINITIONS.

OUTSIDE OF YOURSELF,
WHO DOES THIS HELP?

FIGURE OUT WHAT IT'S FOR.

FIND SOME FORM OF WORK WITH
YOUR HANDS THAT YOU ENJOY.

PEOPLE WHO ASK THE SAME QUESTION
TWICE ARE NOT LOOKING FOR
AN ANSWER, BUT A CONFRONTATION.

HOME REQUIRES A DIFFERENT MIND-SET THAN THE ONE YOU UTILIZE IN THE WORLD. FIND A RELIABLE WAY TO SIGNAL THAT IT IS TIME TO MAKE THIS TRANSITION.

ACT AS THOUGH THE FUTURE YOUR LABOR IS BUILDING IS THE REWARD.

WHEN YOU ARE FEELING STUCK,
TRY WRITING POETRY THAT STICKS
TO A RIGOROUS METER
AND RHYMING PATTERN.

LOOK AT AN OLD PHOTOGRAPH AND
TRY TO IMAGINE THE STATE OF
MIND OF EVERYONE IN THE PHOTO.

WHEN SOMEONE SAYS SOMETHING THAT DOESN'T FIT NEATLY INTO YOUR THINKING, DON'T DISMISS IT OUT OF HAND. INSTEAD, ASK "WHAT IF THEY ARE RIGHT?"

SKIM AN INTERVIEW WITH AN INDIVIDUAL YOU ADMIRE UNTIL YOU COME ACROSS A BOOK OR A MOVIE THEY'VE RECOMMENDED. CONSUME IT WHILE BELIEVING IT IS THE KEY TO THEIR SUCCESS.

SPEND ONE AFTERNOON A MONTH DOING NOTHING MORE THAN SITTING IN YOUR BACKYARD OR A PARK AND WATCHING THE LIFE OCCURRING AROUND YOU.

DON'T EDIT OR JUDGE WHILE YOU ARE CREATING. JUST CREATE. THE TIME FOR EVALUATION WILL COME.

REDUCE THE AMOUNT
OF SPACE IT TAKES UP
UNTIL YOU'RE HAPPY.

RESIST THE URGE TO DISPOSE
OF THINGS, TO DISMISS THEM.

REVIVE YOUR RELIANCE ON INDEX CARDS

ALLOW YOURSELF

TO BE SEEN

DO YOUR BEST TO VALUE
THE TIME OF OTHERS.

BUY MORE FLOWERS. FOR
YOURSELF, AND FOR OTHERS.

TREAT EACH ACTION AS THOUGH IT
WERE FIXED, UNCHANGEABLE, DESTINED.

TURN AN ERRAND
INTO A SPY MISSION.

TAKE CARE OF THE PEOPLE
WHO TAKE CARE OF YOU.

WHO IN YOUR LIFE COULD YOU NOT
STAND BEING PROVEN RIGHT?
USE THAT POSSIBILITY AS FUEL.

INSTEAD OF ASKING FOR
HELP, LOOK AROUND FOR
OPPORTUNITIES WHERE
YOU CAN PROVIDE IT.

FIND A WAY TO GET PAST
THE "NO" IN YOUR MIND AND
SEARCH FOR A SOLUTION.

CHANGE YOUR FORTUNE

CYF

BEING EXCITED IS MORE IMPORTANT THAN BEING INFORMED

CYF

CHANGE YOUR FORTUNE

FIND A MANTRA

IMMEDIATE FONDNESS IS
RARELY A SIGN OF
GREAT THINGS TO COME.

DRILL DOWN UNTIL YOU CAN
IDENTIFY THE ELEMENTS OF
WHAT YOU ARE WORKING ON.

IF SOMEONE'S CRITICISM IS TROUBLING YOU, ASK YOURSELF: IS THERE A CHANCE THIS PERSON IS WRONG NUMEROUS TIMES A DAY? IF THE ANSWER IS YES, ASK YOURSELF WHY THAT WOULDN'T APPLY TO WHAT THEY SAID CONCERNING YOU.

ONCE YOU HAVE A DEADLINE, WRITE OUT WHAT WILL NEED TO HAPPEN EACH DAY IN ORDER TO MEET IT.

ASSUME THAT EVERYTHING WILL TAKE
AT LEAST FOUR TIMES LONGER
THAN YOUR INITIAL ASSESSMENT.

WHEN PREPARING AN ESSAY, ARTICLE,
SPEECH, OR PRESENTATION, KEEP IN
MIND THAT WHILE YOU TAKE TIME
TO WARM UP, YOUR AUDIENCE DOESN'T.

STOP VIEWING YOURSELF
IN TERMS OF OTHERS.

ASSESS HOW DIFFICULT IT IS FOR YOU
TO SAY NO. RECOGNIZE THAT IS THE CASE
FOR EVERYONE, AND GET LESS AFRAID OF
ASKING FOR WHAT YOU WANT AND NEED.

DON'T WORK UP TO THE HARD STUFF,
OR YOU'LL NEVER GET STARTED.
GET IT OUT OF THE WAY IMMEDIATELY.

BE WARY OF ANYONE WHO SALTS THEIR
FOOD WITHOUT TASTING IT FIRST.

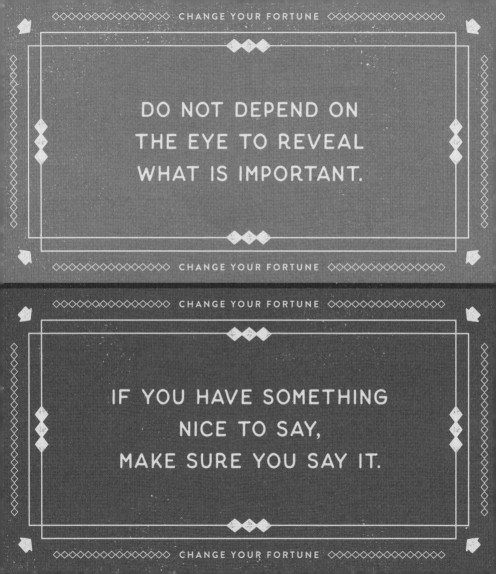